COMMON SENSE SUPERVISION

COMMON SENSE SUPERVISION

A HANDBOOK FOR SUCCESS
AS A SUPERVISOR

by ROGER FULTON

TEN SPEED PRESS
BERKELEY, CALIFORNIA

Copyright © 1988 by Knight Management Company

Knight Management Corporation
P.O. Box 12035
Albany, New York 12212

1🜚

TEN SPEED PRESS
P.O. Box 7123
Berkeley, California 94707
www.tenspeed.com

Distributed in Australia by Simon and Schuster Australia, in Canada by Ten Speed Press Canada, in New Zealand by Tandem Press, in South Africa by Real Books, in Southeast Asia by Berkeley Books, and in the United Kingdom and Europe by Airlift Books.

Cover design by Fifth Street Design
Book design by Stephen Herold
Typesetting by Lasergraphics

Library of Congress Cataloging-in-Publication Data

Fulton, Roger
      Common-sense supervision: a handbook for success as a supervisor
      / by Roger Fulton
          p.   cm.
      ISBN 0-89815-258-5
      1. Supervision of employees—Handbooks, manuals, etc. I. Title.
HF549.12.F85 1988
658.3'02—dc19   88—24811
                                                         CIP

Printed in Canada

8 9 10 — 02 01 00 99 98

TABLE OF CONTENTS

❦ CHAPTER ONE: INTRODUCTION

"Common Sense is instinct, and enough of it is genius."
Josh Billings

CAN I BE A SUCCESSFUL SUPERVISOR?

*T*HE ANSWER to that question is that most people *can* succeed as a supervisor. But, just as with success in anything, it will require knowledge, training, experience and a great deal of effort on your part. Other people can help you, but it is *you* who must put forth the effort to succeed.

In addition to having the common sense to pick up this book, you already have completed several steps toward your success.

1. Your superiors already have faith in your abilities to be a supervisor since they have given you that title.
2. You probably already have a great deal of knowledge and experience in your own industry which can give you insight into future problems and solutions.
3. You already have a positive attitude toward your work and your company since you have put forth the effort to be successful in your career thus far.

1

Given these assets, it should not be difficult for you to build on them and to reach true success as a supervisor of others.

FACE THE FACTS

Supervising the work activities of other people can be a rewarding and satisfying experience. It can give you the opportunity to coordinate the activities of several people, or several groups of people, and to ultimately see the fruits of their efforts turn into a fully developed final product. One which no single person could produce alone.

In order to ultimately experience the satisfaction and rewards of your position, you must also experience the difficulties and the frustrations of dealing with your employees. Their problems, frustrations and failures can result in trying times for both of you. Helping both of you to avoid, or work through, those trying times is the purpose of this book.

YOU ARE NOT ALONE

Dozens of ideas, proven concepts and solutions are presented on the following pages. They are presented in a practial, concise, common sense form so that you can start using them tomorrow to be the best supervisor that you can be. It should be noted, however, that this text does not tell you how to handle *every* situation. That would be impossible since every situation, every employee and every supervisor is different.

Given this, the key to successful supervision is *your* ability to handle the unique and unusual situations which will confront you throughout your career. The material contained in this book will give you guidelines to follow for success, but it is you, and you alone, who must use these guidelines, and your own common sense, when handling each new and challenging situation.

❦ CHAPTER 2: YOU AND THE ORGANIZATION

"No man is an island, entire of itself; every man is a piece of the continent, a part of the main."

John Donne

YOUR ROLE

*A*s a supervisor, you are responsible for the activities and performance of others, not just for your own performance.

Your job is now less defined with more gray areas.

Your time will be at a premium. Initially, you will feel that there are barely enough hours in the day to get everything done.

You will tend to take the job home with you more—not just paperwork, but the problems of the day as well.

You must learn to be a buffer between your own supervisors and your employees. Both sides have their own goals, desires and needs. Your job is to keep them both reasonably happy and satisfied while *keeping yourself happy and satisfied* as well.

Sound difficult? A little overwhelming? Relax!

It's easier than you think and it is well worth the effort.

"The executive exists to make sensible exceptions to general rules."

Elting E. Morison

EXECUTIVE PRIVILEGES

Even if you are not a true "Executive," the quality of your life has substantially increased by becoming a supervisor.

People will have more respect for you since you have advanced in your job.

Your paycheck will go up considerably.

You will probably be getting better fringe benefits; more insurance, longer vacations.

You will be treated much better by upper level management. You'll have better access to the boss and you'll be able to assist in policy-making decisions.

Enjoy those benefits!

You have earned them and you will continue to earn them, *everyday.*

> *"Each honest calling, each walk of life, has its own elite, its own aristocracy based upon excellence of performance."*
> James Bryant Conant

GETTING ALONG WITH THE BOSS

This is priority *one!* He/she can make your life very difficult or very easy.

Here are a few rules to follow:

1. Don't take up too much of his/her time; just enough to get the information and guidance you need.
2. Don't be afraid of the boss. The boss needs you as much as you need the boss. Remember that their job is to get things done through people—and you are one of those people.
3. Keep in mind that all bosses are people and all people have quirks. Therefore, all bosses have quirks. Learn them and heed them. It'll be to your advantage.
4. Never embarrass the boss; intentionally or accidentally.

If you can get along with the boss, you've gone a long way toward success as a supervisor.

> *"He who has never learned to obey, cannot be a good commander."*
>
> Aristotle

THE INFORMAL ORGANIZATION

Defined: This is the underground! The informal employee power structure. It is made up of regular workers who are respected by other workers for their experience, their knowledge or their connections. They control the pipeline for the informal rumors and information among the employees.

Handle this informal organization, or it will handle you. It can make you or break you depending on what is said by you and about you.

How do you handle it? By being fair and up front with all of your employees, with specific attention to the informal leaders. Just treat them right in their jobs and let them know what's going on—informally, of course. Then they will spread the truth about you and the organization rather than circulating false rumors and innuendos.

If you're fair to all, you'll fare well.

> *"The first and great commandment is: Don't let them scare you."*
>
> Elmer Davis

MORALE

Morale can be affected positively or negatively by an incident which seems insignificant to you, but which may be very important to your employees.

A happy crew will do more and better work than an unhappy crew.

Rumors and unfairness are the enemies of good morale.

If there is unfair treatment of one employee, they will all feel that they may be next in line for this unfair treatment.

If you know what is going on in your department, you can straighten out misunderstandings or dispel false rumors *before* they adversely affect employee morale.

A high level of employee morale is your ultimate goal. Following the priciples set out in future pages will assist you in achieving this goal.

Keep in mind that subordinates of *excellent leaders* have *excellent morale*. Subordinates of *poor leaders* have *poor morale*.

> *"Abuse a man unjustly, and you will make friends for him."*
>
> Edgar Watson Howe

ESPRIT DE CORPS

This means the employees' pride in their work and in the organization.

Outside recognition for excellent performance, whether from the media, other organizations, professional associations or your own organization will lead to excellent esprit de corps.

As a supervisor, you should seek out these types of awards for your people and strive for the excellence to obtain them. Let them know you are seeking to obtain them, not for you, but for them, because *they* deserve it.

In the everyday environment, encourage them to do their collective best to perform as a team—*the best team*—in the business.

They will feel better about themselves and work better for you and the organization.

> *"Destiny is not a matter of chance, it is a matter of choice;*
> *it is nothing to be waited for, it is a thing to be achieved."*
> William Jennings Bryan

INTERNAL CONFLICT

Stay in your own domain!

You will have enough to do with your own job. Don't try to meddle in another department's affairs unless your failure to take action will adversely affect your department's performance!

Resolve interdepartmental conflicts with your equal in the other department. If you have given them the opportunity to resolve it informally between the two of you, and have met with unreasonable resistance, then you are justified in advising your superior and having him assist in resolving the problem.

Carefully choose which battles you are willing to fight. Not all battles are worth the resulting bad feelings or long term problems that will result, even if you win. However, some are!

You get paid for your judgment! Use it wisely!

"Strive mightily, but eat and drink as friends."
William Shakespeare

COMPETITION FROM PEERS

This is related to what you just read.

The organizational structure is a pyramid and it gets narrow at the top.

When several good people (you and your peers), vie for the next highest level in the pyramid, there can be very stiff competition.

Protect yourself at all times!

Don't get pushed around, but don't look for trouble either.

In the heat of the competition, don't be a "back-stabber" or an "endrunner." Both of these will cost you dearly in the end.

Your best overall strategy in the competition is to be loyal, mind your own business and do your job to the best of your ability.

You'll come out a true winner in the long haul!

> *"I studied the lives of great men and famous women, and I found that the men and women who got to the top were those who did the jobs they had in hand, with everything they had of energy and enthusiasm and hard work."*
>
> Harry S. Truman

This is the end of Chapter Two:
See how easy it was?
Now that you have a good idea about the forces within the organization and their relationship to you, let's turn to what you should be doing as a first rate supervisor.

> *"There is more credit and satisfaction in being a first rate truck driver than being a tenth-rate executive."*
>
> B. C. Forbes

"A competent leader can get efficient service from poor troops; while on the contrary, an incapable leader can demoralize the best troops."

General John S. Pershing

SET THE EXAMPLE

*S*HOW UP on time; or, preferably, early.

Dress appropriately for your business.

Don't do personal business on company time.

Don't spend an hour reading the newspaper, drinking coffee or goofing off. *Get right to your job.*

Gossip, sour grapes, complaining and laziness have no place in a supervisor's office.

Your conduct, appearance, attitudes and work habits will set the tone for your employees conduct, appearance, attitude and work habits.

In short, be a model employee and others will pattern themselves after you.

"Always do right; this will gratify some people and astonish the rest."

Mark Twain

BE TECHNICALLY PROFICIENT

Know your job!

You probably have a good technical background in your industry or you would not have been chosen to be a supervisor.

However, when it comes to being a supervisor, the technical problems are usually easy. It's the *people problems* that can cause the greatest difficulty.

You already have the right idea though because you are reading this book. However, this is only a guide on supervision. It does not contain everything you will ever need to know about your whole job.

Attend technical seminars to keep current in this rapidly changing technological age. Attend management seminars to hone your personal management skills.

A progressive organization will welcome your initiative and will usually pay the expenses of such education.

How can you go wrong?

> *"He who has no inclination to learn more will be very apt to think that he knows enough."*
>
> Powell

MAKE A DECISION!

The worst decision is no decision.

In order for a decision to be worthwhile, it must be sound and made in a timely fashion.

The people above you have faith in your ability to make decisions or they would not have made you a supervisor.

However, as we all know, not all decisions are good decisions. But if they are based on the following process, they should never be bad decisions.

When a decision must be made:

1. Gather all the facts you need to understand the situation.
2. Analyze the facts and review them objectively.
3. Formulate possible strategies and consider the consequences of each.
4. Choose the best one and make the decision to implement it.

Some decisions are made in seconds, some in days and some in months. However, they all are made the same way.

If you can't make a decision, or consistently make the wrong one, then being a supervisor is not for you and you should choose another career path.

"Nothing is more difficult, and therefore more precious, than to be able to decide."

Napoleon

TAKE RESPONSIBILITY FOR YOUR ACTIONS

This means right or wrong!

Don't try to pass the buck, it stops at your desk.

If you made a decision based on the process outlined on the last page, then stand by that decision and cite the reasons why you made that decision.

If your supervisor says your decision was wrong and must be changed, then *it is no longer your decision.* It is *their decision* and *they* must take the responsibility for it.

Chances are that you will seldom be called wrong by a good supervisor. Usually, they will let your decision stand. If it wasn't the best alternative, then they will give you a chance to modify your decision, but not necessarily change it.

Keep in mind that your boss understands the decision-making process and has to rely on you in the future. He understands that you will not be perfect every time. If you were, he couldn't afford you.

One last point on this. Seldom will success or failure depend on one simple decision. If you are right, or nearly right, the majority of the time in decision making, you will be considered successful.

> *"We do our best that we know how at the moment, and if it doesn't turn out, we modify it."*
>
> Franklin D. Roosevelt

KNOW YOURSELF

There is not one among us who is perfect in every way and in every situation.

However, by knowing your own strengths and weaknesses, you can *maximize your strengths* and *minimize your weaknesses.*

Once you know and understand yourself, the business of knowing and understanding others will bc much easier.

> *"When a man points a finger at someone else, he should remember that four of his fingers are pointing at himself."*
> Louis Nizer

MAINTAIN A POSITIVE ATTITUDE

Your success and the success of your employees will both depend on your attitude. If it is a positive attitude toward your work and the organization's goals, then your actions and words will convey that to your employees.

If you convey a negative attitude, then the employees will key on your "negativeness."

If you are to maintain a healthy and productive atmosphere in the workplace, you must have a healthy and productive attitude toward your work and your organization.

"Man is what he believes."
Anton Chekhov

HANDLE PERSONAL STRESS

Is being a supervisor stressful? YES! Is that stress harmful to you? Not necessarily!

It's all in how *you* handle it.

Be concerned and conscientious, but don't be a worrier.

The organization was here before you got here and will be here long after you are gone!

Do the best you can to maintain and improve the organization, but don't constantly worry about every little thing or you will destroy yourself and be of no value to anyone.

Accept those things that you cannot change; but change those things that you can.

> *"To accept whatever comes, regardless of the consequences, is to be unafraid."*
>
> John Cage

GIVE ORDERS PROPERLY

Many supervisors fall miserably in this area.

Here are some simple guidelines:

In routine matters—"Could you...," "Would you...," "As soon as you get a chance..." etc.

In emergency or high priority situations, direct orders are appropriate—"Do...," "Go...," "Handle this immediately..." etc.

Naturally, a simple "Please" followed by a "Thank you" is nearly always appropriate.

> *"What you cannot enforce, do not command."*
> Sophocles

DON'T EXPECT *TOO* MUCH

Ensure that the quantity and quality of the work you expect is set at a *reasonable* level.

If people are pushed beyond their limits for an extended period of time, they will burn out and productivity will decrease just when you need it most. By setting *reasonable* standards, you can be sure that you will still have employees who can, and will, work harder to meet an unexpected deadline on occasion.

> *"A good horse should be seldom spurred."*
> Thomas Fuller

MAINTAIN YOUR SENSE OF HUMOR

When things go wrong as they sometimes will;
and all your life seems all uphill;
When your career is crumbling,
and production is tumbling;
Stop and reflect that despite your best;
how funny you look in all that mess!

Maintaining your sense of humor will carry you through some of the most difficult times in your career.

Your failure to maintain your sense of humor could end your career quickly if you allow your frustration to build to the breaking point without relief.

"You grow up the day you have the first real laugh— at yourself."

Ethel Barrymore

Stop here and reflect for a few minutes on these last few pages.

Ask yourself these questions:

Are you a good example for your people to follow?
Are you as good as you can be?
Can you make a sound and timely decision based on the facts?
Do you care about your people?

If the answer to all of these questions was "yes," then you are well on your way to being a successful supervisor. Turn the page and continue!

If the answer to any of these questions was "no," take a few more minutes, or longer, and make a commitment to improve in that weak area. Once committed, then turn the page!

*F*EW PEOPLE CAN actually define respect. But we know who we do respect and who we don't respect.

The following pages should help you to be a supervisor that your employees *will* respect.

> *"The leader must know, must know that he knows, and must be able to make it abundantly clear to those about him that he knows."*
>
> Clarence B. Randall

BE BUSINESSLIKE

Always be a professional in every way.
Look like you know what your are doing.
Be together, not rumpled or ruffled.
Don't engage in horseplay or practical jokes.
Don't use obscene or vulgar language; it's demeaning to you.

Rumors
Sexism
Racism
Ethnic Jokes
Obscenities
Practical Jokes
Sarcasm
Gossip

None of these have any place in the workplace.

If you want to be respected, BE A PROFESSIONAL!

"Those who command themselves, command others."
Anonymous

MAINTAIN A GOOD PERSONAL APPEARANCE

Be neat!
Look disciplined!

Keep your weight under control.
Keep your hair cut and well groomed.
Be clean-shaven (men).
Wear enough makeup, but not too much (women).

Wear appropriate business attire for your particular industry.
Look like a professional and set the example.

> *"A man, in order to establish himself in the world, does everything he can to appear established there."*
> La Rochefoucauld

MAINTAIN DISCIPLINE

Don't tolerate disrespect or laziness!

Be sure that your people know the rules, understand the quality and quantity of the work that is required, and that they must maintain the standard of conduct you expect them to maintain.

Then, enforce the rules with a fair and just hand, equally for all.

Maintaining a high, but not unreasonable level of discipline, will save you many problems in the future.

The ultimate compliment for a supervisor is to be known by his people as *"firm but fair."*

That is your ultimate goal!

> *"The superior man is firm in the right way, not merely firm."*
> Confucius

EXHIBIT PERSONAL INTEGRITY

No kickbacks, no favors, no lies, no misleading.

If you engage in any of the above, it will come back to haunt you when you least expect it!

Keep in mind that your employees observe you and your conduct every day. They know more of your business than you think they do.

If they are to have respect for you, your personal integrity must be above reproach.

"The measure of a man's real character is what he would do if he knew he never would be found out."
Thomas Macauloy

HANDLE FRIENDSHIPS
WITH SUBORDINATES CAREFULLY

Very carefully!!

As a supervisor, you are in a different position than you were in your previous position.

Those persons worth having as friends will understand the difference between on duty and off duty familiarity and will respect it!

Those persons not worthy as friends will try to use off duty familiarity to gain an advantage when on duty.

One cardinal rule that you must *never* violate is that: Romance has *no* place in the workplace!!

> *"In a social order where one member is officially subordinate to another, the superior, if he is a gentleman, never thinks of it; and the subordinate, if he is a gentleman, never forgets it."*
>
> General John J. Pershing

TAKE PERSONAL RESPONSIBILITY FOR ERRORS

You are the boss!

If your subordinates perform well, then you have performed well.

If they do not perform well, then you have not performed well.

Don't try to place the blame on others.

You are the supervisor and you are ultimately responsible for everything your people do, good or bad. You cannot shirk this responsibility.

If a mistake occurs, correct the errors and take the steps necessary to ensure that it doesn't happen again.

Then go on from there.

"To be nobly wrong is more manly than to be meanly right."
Thomas Paine

BE PATIENT AND CALM

Use self control at all times.

When things are not going well, it is up to you to find a sound, rational solution.

You can only do that if you are thinking clearly and rationally.

If an emergency arises, others will look to you for guidance and an end to the problem solution.

If you are not in control of yourself, you become a part of the problem, not a part of the solution.

"In all good things, reason should prevail."
William Penn

BE CONSISTENT

Don't enforce the rules today and ignore them tomorrow!

People are content in knowing what is expected from them and they adjust to the rules even when the rules and the enforcement are strict.

Therefore, don't be erratic, or your employees will not know what is truly expected of them.

Your inconsistency will translate into employee disciplinary problems and an uneasy feeling throughout your department.

Consistency is critical to your success as a supervisor.

> *"Nothing that isn't a real crime makes a man appear so contemptible and little in the eyes of the world as inconsistency."*
>
> Joseph Addison

EXPECT GOOD CONDUCT

Don't tolerate dangerous horseplay or dangerous or demeaning practical jokes.

A little good clean fun is often good for morale, but be sure it's not overdone.

Employees will learn the limits and will conform their conduct to those limits.

Failure to maintain this standard can result in serious consequences for you, the employees, and your organization in the form of complaints, injuries and, eventually, lawsuits.

> *"In every real man, a child is hidden that wants to play."*
> Friedrich Nietzsche

EXPECT GOOD WORK

If it isn't done right, tell the employee what is wrong with it, the right way to do it, and have them do it correctly.

If it still isn't done correctly after that, keep returning it until it is done correctly.

Maintain your standards of excellence at all times.

Your employees will know what standard is expected of them and will perform to that standard accordingly.

If you allow shoddy work then *that* will become the *standard* of your department over time!

> *"The difference between failure and success is doing a thing nearly right and doing a thing exactly right."*
>
> Edward Simmons

ACKNOWLEDGE GOOD WORK WITH PRAISE

Don't praise just to praise, but let your employees know you care and that you noticed their efforts.

The thought that a person works for money alone has been disproved by innumerable researchers.

The most satisfying reason for a person to work is that it makes that person feel worthwhile and that he/she is making a contribution to some larger effort.

Recognition of a worker's personal efforts will pay dividends a thousand times to you and to the organization.

> *"A pat on the back is only a few vertebrae removed from a kick in the pants, but is miles ahead in results."*
>
> V. Wilcox

PRAISE IN PUBLIC/CHASTISE IN PRIVATE

This is a cardinal rule! Don't ever forget it!
Anything said in public, becomes public.

There is no need to embarrass an employee in front of his peers or other supervisors.

If it is necessary to chastise an employee for poor work or conduct, the privacy of your office is the place to do it.

However, if an employee has performed in an excellent manner, you can make him a proud individual by praising his/her efforts in the presence of co-workers.

> *"I have yet to find a man, however exalted his station, who did not do better work and put forth greater effort under a spirit of approval than under a spirit of criticism."*
>
> Charles Schwarz

AVOID UNNECESSARY ACTIVITY

Don't "make work."

If goals are set and employees work hard to finish early, don't ruin it by forcing them to do extra unnecessary extra work.

Keep paperwork to a minimum. Very few people enjoy doing paperwork. If they view it as redundant, they will resent it even more.

You can plan in advance for slow periods by arranging for vacation time or personal time off for employees during non-peak periods to avoid having to keep employees "busy" during these times.

Your planning ahead will show you as a capable manager and will be benefit you, the employees and the organization.

> *"It is not enough to be busy…the question is: what are we busy about?"*
>
> Henry David Thoreau

KNOW WHAT IS GOING ON

Don't sit in your office all day!

You won't learn anything except what somebody wants you to know.

Practice "MBWA"—Management By Walking Around.

Get out and talk to your people. They will tell you what is really happening, either directly or by dropping hints.

You can gauge morale, prevent potential problems and develop an open dialogue with your employees by spending time with them.

In your travels, don't forget to talk to other supervisors and the upper level management so you can get the "big picture" and anticipate future demands on your department.

> *"It takes a great man to make a good listener."*
> Sir Arthur Helps

BE IMPARTIAL

Treat everyone equally!
Don't play favorites!
Set personal prejudices aside!
In some ways, you are like a judge in a court. You must resolve employee conflicts. You must balance production concerns and people concerns. You must balance labor concerns and management concerns.

In order to do this effectively, and with the support of all parties, you must be recognized as an impartial judge of the facts in order to be successful.

"Unless justice be done to others, it will not be done to us."
Woodrow Wilson

❦ CHAPTER FIVE: WINNING CONFIDENCE

*I*F YOUR PEOPLE don't have confidence in you, then they will isolate you from their problems and ignore you when they need a solution. Ultimately, you will have no idea what is going on and no control over what is.

The following pages contain a few simple rules for gaining the confidence of your employees.

"Lead, follow or get out of the way!"
Col. Harold P. Knutty

APPEAR CONFIDENT

Look like you know what you are doing (even when you have doubts).

The best way to appear confident is to have faith in yourself and your capabilities. The best way to have faith in your capabilities is to be knowledgeable, experienced and be able to systematically work through any problem in a calm and efficient manner.

> *"The world is governed more by appearances than by realities, so that it is fully as necessary to seem to know something as to know it."*
>
> Daniel Webster

BE AVAILABLE

You must make time for your people; they are your most valuable resource.

Communication is an art with many flaws. Even though you try to make things perfectly clear through oral and written orders, there are times when employees need a decision or the answer to a simple question to properly complete the task at hand.

If you are not available for consultation, then the project may not continue in the proper direction. If it goes in the wrong direction, you have wasted a great deal of time, effort and money; all for the want of a short consultation with you for clarification or guidance.

> *"Every great mistake has a halfway moment, a split second when it can be recalled and perhaps remedied."*
>
> Pearl S. Buck

ENCOURAGE FREE SPEECH

If your employees don't talk to you, they'll talk to each other and leave you in the dark.

If you know about a problem, you can handle it. If you don't know, then it can only get worse and you will have no control over it.

Many grievances are resolved just by bringing the problem to the attention of the boss, whether or not he/she can do anything about it.

Listen to new ideas; consider them on their merits, and implement those that can benefit the employees, the department or the organization.

"Words are the best medium of exchange of thoughts and ideas between people."

William Ross

KEEP YOUR PEOPLE INFORMED

There are very few necessary secrets in most industries.

Keeping your employees informed of what is going on in the organization eliminates unfounded rumors and lets them understand the bigger picture.

If you keep them accurately informed, they will learn to come to you for the facts—and will learn to trust you in the process.

"Nothing is so burdensome as a secret."
French Proverb

INSIST ON HONESTY

Don't tolerate lies or deceitful conduct.

Investigate, develop facts and directly confront anyone who is deceitful or who openly lies to cover up a problem.

Words will quickly spread that you don't tolerate dishonesty among your employees.

This "up front" policy will benefit you in handling problem situations and will ultimately benefit the entire organization as well.

> *"Hateful of me as the Gates of Hades is that man who hides one thing in his heart and speaks another."*
>
> Homer

KEEP PROMISES!

Or don't make them!

Promise to try; but don't promise what you can't guarantee.

In the same vein, if you promise a subordinate that you will perform a certain task for them, then be sure to do it. And do it in a timely fashion.

By doing so, they will learn to trust you and will learn to have confidence in you, your word, and your ability to get things done.

> *"Who breaks his faith, no faith is held with him."*
> Seigneur Du Bartas

GIVE CREDIT FOR IDEAS

It makes employees feel good and builds up morale to know that they had input into a decision or product.

If you steal their ideas and claim they are yours, it will be noticed.

Result? They'll never come up with an idea again. At least not one that you'll hear about!

"The most powerful factors in the world are clear ideas in the minds of energetic men of good will."
J. Arthur Thomson

DON'T CRITICIZE SUPERIORS

Just as you have to make decisions in your position, your supervisors have to make their decisions. Even if you don't agree with a superior's decision, it is your responsibility to implement that decision.

Criticizing your supervisor's decisions in front of your people serves no purpose. The fact that you were critical will get back to your supervisors and they will realize that you cannot be relied on to support them.

Your days will then be numbered in your organization.

> *"Loyalty is the one thing a leader cannot do without."*
> A. P. Gouthey

RESPECT THE CONFIDENCE OF SUBORDINATES

Never gossip!

If an employee tells you something in confidence, then keep it in confidence.

If word gets out that you violated a subordinate's trust, the communication between you and all of your employees is dead forever!

> *"If once you forfeit the confidence of your fellow citizens,*
> *you can never regain their respect and esteem."*
>
> Abraham Lincoln

❦CHAPTER SIX: WINNING LOYALTY

"Too often a sense of loyalty depends on admiration, and if we can't admire, it is difficult to be loyal."
Aimee Buchanan

BE PLEASANT

*T*REAT OTHERS as you would like to be treated. Being pleasant is easy and it doesn't cost you anything!

Keeping the work environment comfortable for your subordinates will make them want to come to work and they'll enjoy their stay more while they are there.

This will ultimately translate into increased productivity within your department as a direct result of your "friendly" demeanor.

"Be pleasant until 10 o'clock in the morning and the rest of the day will take care of itself."
Elbert Hubbard

KNOW YOUR PEOPLE

Your people are your most valuable asset. However, they are individual people, not objects.

Get to know their hobbies and interests.

Ask about their families, their health, their vacation.

They'll know that you care about them as people—not just as employees.

Learn their strengths and their weaknesses. You will then be able to steer them in the right direction when assigning work so they can maximize their own potential.

In assigning them tasks that allow them to use their talents and abilities, without exceeding their capabilities, you will develop a satisfied and loyal employee.

> *"There is no meaning to life except the meaning man gives his life by the unfolding of his powers."*
>
> Erich Fromm

HELP YOUR PEOPLE TO DO THEIR JOBS

Make their work easier for them through training, experience or new technology.

Be sure that they have all of the proper tools to do their jobs to the best of their abilities.

Eliminate any stumbling blocks to the successful completion of their tasks which may come from other departments, unreasonable restrictions or deadlines, or a lack of proper resources.

And, of course, give them the encouragement they need to successfully complete difficult or lengthy tasks.

> *"So much of what we call management consists of making it difficult for people to work."*
>
> Peter Drucker

TRAIN YOUR PEOPLE

They can't do a good job for you unless they know how!

Show them the proper way of doing the job they are assigned to do. Tell them what you expect in regard to productivity. Take time with them until they have learned the job thoroughly.

After that, teach them new or easier ways of doing their jobs.

Encourage them to learn new skills, either on or off the job.

In fact, arrange for it by making them aware of schools, seminars, training sessions and new technology.

Learning new skills will keep them from becoming stagnant. It will lead to your being able to rely on them for new projects or increased responsibility.

Training is beneficial to them, to you, and to the organization.

"To teach is to learn."
Japanese Proverb

DEVELOP YOUR PEOPLE

Take time to talk to them about their futures.

Give them the benefit of your experience and advise them on how to succeed in their careers.

If they show talent in a particular area, assist them in gaining additional knowledge and experience in that area.

Give them added responsibility gradually. Build up their confidence and ability.

The time you spend will pay dividends in their increased performance—now and in the future!

After all, didn't someone during your career take the time to talk to you, train you and tell you how to be successful?

> *"Few things help an individual more than to place responsibility upon him, and to let him know that you trust him."*
> Booker T. Washington

WATCH OUT FOR YOUR PEOPLE

Protect them from unreasonable rules or poor decisions which adversely affect them.

Assist them in obtaining their medical and dental benefits, tuition assistance, special training, etc.

Help them get time off when they need it for personal affairs.

If they make an error, help to minimize the effect of that error. That will also minimize the consequences they may face, i.e. disciplinary action or a poor performance rating.

If you watch out for your employees, they will watch out for you.

> *"You must be able to underwrite the honest mistakes of your subordinates if you wish to develop their initiative and experience."*
>
> General Bruce C. Clarke

MAINTAIN SAFETY STANDARDS

Protect your people.

Keep safety equipment available and in good working condition. Ensure that your people know how to use it properly.

Enforce the safety rules rigidly.

The supervisor who forges ahead to meet production quotas at the expense of the safety of his people, clearly shows his employees that he doesn't care about them as people.

If you don't care about *them*, do you think they will care about *you?*

> *"If you are out of trouble, watch for danger."*
> Sophocles

BE UNDERSTANDING

Try to understand your subordinates' problems. Listen to them.

You are not just a boss, you are the symbol of something stronger and, they feel, wiser than they are.

Therefore, they will value your opinion in all matters.

Assist them whenever you can by listening and/or counselling. They will often solve their own problems, answer their own questions and make their own decisions, sometimes without your having to say a word.

> *"To say the right thing at the right time, keep still most of the time."*
>
> John W. Roper

THE VALUE OF LOYALTY

The dedication of your employees can be critical to your future success within your organization.

Never forget that, as you go higher in the organization, many of your best employees will also go higher in the organization.

The old adage: "Surround Thyself With Competence," may take on new meaning when you need competent and dedicated employees to support you when you go on to a new position.

The loyalties built up in the past can be invaluable in the future under many circumstances!

"Be nice to people on your way up because you may meet them on your way down."

Anonymous

❦ CHAPTER SEVEN: PREVENTING AND HANDLING PROBLEMS

$\mathcal{A}$LL PROBLEMS can be handled!—No matter how difficult they appear to be!

Your ability to foresee, prevent and handle problems can be a true test of your ability as a supervisor.

The following pages will assist you in handling this sometimes difficult area of supervision.

> *"These are the times that try men's souls."*
> Thomas Paine

ACTIVELY SUPERVISE

Check on *everything* periodically!

You can rest assured that the area you don't check will be the source of the next crisis.

Don't always take another's word for things. Get out of your office and double-check things.

It's nice to trust, but you also have to be sure that your trust is well placed.

> *"Modest doubt is called the beacon of the wise."*
> William Shakespeare

ENSURE THAT THE GOALS ARE UNDERSTOOD

Tell your employees what you want, then have them tell you what you want.

Follow-up with written orders, then check to see that they understand the written orders.

Check the progress being made on the project periodically to be sure it is being done according to the intent of your directives.

Communication is an inexact art.

However, making the communication as clear as possible will enhance performance and minimize errors.

> *"It is less dishonour to hear imperfectly, than to speak imperfectly."*
>
> Ben Johnson

ANTICIPATE PROBLEM AREAS

"An ounce of prevention is worth a pound of cure."
And so it is with problems.
Look ahead! — What areas could cause difficulties?

Possibly:

New employees
Poor training
Inexperience
Poor quality materials
Too much; too fast—of anything!

You can't see into the future, but you can project the ramifications of certain factors on the success of a project.

Correct as many deficiencies as possible before they cause problems.

> *"It isn't that they can't see the solution. It is that they can't see the problem."*
>
> G. K. Chesterton

DO SOMETHING!

Don't ignore a problem!

Don't try to hide it! — Handle it!

Correct the problem and take steps to ensure it doesn't become a problem again in the future.

Many supervisors fail in this area. "The buck stops here" should be a phrase that all supervisors should live by.

Many problems which could have been solved with a small amount of supervisory intervention have been ignored until they ultimately escalated into a serious problem for employees, managers and the organization.

Don't let it happen to you!

> *"Facts do not cease to exist because they are ignored."*
> Aldous Huxley

INVESTIGATE

Get all the facts about the problem that has occurred and identify the factors leading up to it.

Interview the affected or involved employees. Get their ideas on what happened, why it occurred and how it could have been prevented.

Back up the interviews with physical evidence whenever possible. Check every source of information you can think of.

Once you gather all of the facts and you look at the whole picture, you can take sound and logical steps to correct the problem and prevent a reoccurrence.

> *"To solve a problem, it is necessary to think. It is necessary to think even to decide what facts to collect."*
> Robert Maynard Hutchins

DO YOUR HOMEWORK

After you investigate to find the cause of the problem, you can formulate possible solutions.

Take time to analyze the solutions and project what effects these possible solutions will have on your department, other departments and the organization as a whole.

Once you "do your homework" in this area, you will see things more logically and clearly and—you'll have the answers for the boss!

> *"If a man takes no thought about what is distant, he will find sorrow near at hand."*
>
> Confucius

BE CREATIVE

Turn adversity into opportunity!

When problems occur, the most important task for a supervisor is to get it corrected so the operation can return to normal as soon as possible.

However, don't stop there! Stand back and look at the problem objectively. Ask yourself questions such as "How could this have been prevented?" or "What can I learn from this?"

The answers may surprise you.

Perhaps the incident will give you the support you need to get new equipment or increased training for your employees.

Creative thinking can lead to creative solutions!

> *"Creativeness often consists of merely turning up what is already there."*
>
> Bernie Fitz-Gibbon

DOCUMENT YOUR ACTIONS

Put it on paper:

How the problem came to your attention.
What investigation you did.
What was the cause.
What steps you took to solve it.
What you did to prevent reoccurrence.

Take the time to write it down and keep it on file.
It will prove invaluable weeks or months later in:

Employee disciplinary hearings.
Employee ratings.
Your rating.
Lawsuits.

> *"The memorandum is written, not so much to inform the reader, as it is to protect the writer."*
>
> Anonymous

DON'T EMBARRASS THE BOSS

Keep *your* supervisor informed!

Nothing could be more embarrassing than your supervisor's supervisor asking for the status of a particular problem when your supervisor has no idea that the problem even exists.

Periodically keep your supervisor informed of the status of your investigation into the problem area and your preliminary findings.

When you have completed your investigation, corrected the problem and have recommendations for preventing future occurrences, contact your supervisor again.

He/she will appreciate your follow-up work and will know that there is no need for further action on their part.

"The past at least is secure."
Daniel Webster

❦ CHAPTER EIGHT: ADMINISTRATION

*A*LONG WITH BEING a supervisor, you are also an administrator. It goes with the territory.

On the following pages you will find a few tips on "administrative survival."

> *"Bad administration, to be sure, can destroy good policy."*
> Adlai Stevenson

WRITE IT DOWN

You now have too many things on your mind to rely solely on your memory.

If you don't write things down, you're going to forget to be somewhere or do something and that will reflect adversely on you and cause problems for others.

A simple daily or weekly calendar will help keep track of appointments, events and deadlines.

Of course, you always have to remember to look at the calendar regularly, too!

"Quite literally, a man's memory is what he forgets with."
Odell Shepard

GET ORGANIZED

When you can't find the last marketing report, the vacation schedule, shipping papers or anything else in less than five minutes, you are in serious trouble. Continue in that pattern, and soon you won't need to find anything—at least not at that job.

Take time to get organized, but not to the point of being a fanatic about it.

With a little thought, planning and self-discipline, you can make effective use of daily scheduling guides, file folders, in and out baskets, commercial planning systems, computers and a whole host of other items designed to make your job easier.

Consider time spent getting organized—and staying organized—as job insurance.

> *"Let all things be done decently and in order."*
> Corinthians 14:40

MANAGE RESOURCES EFFECTIVELY

You are responsible for the effective and efficient utilization of the resources at your disposal. This includes material, equipment and the most valuable of all resources, the employees.

Ensure that you have enough resources to get the job done. Plan ahead so you have enough people, material and equipment, all at the right time, and in the right place, to get the job done.

In addition, your job is to prevent the waste of valuable resources. This includes time as well as materials. Proper planning, coupled with proper supervision, will ensure that all resources are used effectively.

"Nothing is more terrible than activity without insight."
Thomas Carlyle

KEEP GOOD RECORDS

Production records, overtime usage, attendance records, employee performance records, supply orders, equipment accountability. These are just a few of the records you may be required to keep as a supervisor.

They are as necessary to the control of a business as laws are to an orderly society. Accept the fact that they must be kept and that you must keep them as accurately as possible.

You will find that, with proper organization and forethought on your part, they are not all that difficult to keep.

Many supervisors fail in this area because they continually put record keeping low on their list of priorities. Subsequently, this activity builds up into an overwhelming, time consuming task.

Keeping good records on a daily or weekly basis, a little at a time, will make this activity—and your job—much easier.

> *"Order marches with weighty and measured strides; disorder is always in a hurry."*
>
> Napoleon

DELEGATE

You can't do everything yourself.

You have to delegate some tasks to other competent people. Not just menial tasks, but meaningful tasks as well.

Be sure that the person you delegate the task to has the ability to perform the task.

Then, trust them. Give them an assignment and the authority to carry it out.

But remember the cardinal rule of delegation!

You can delegate authority, but not responsibility. You are responsible for the end result!

> *"Treat people as if they were what they ought to be and you help them become what they are capable of being."*
> Johann W. Von Goethe

DEVELOP PERSONAL CONTACTS

Just as people can create a myriad of problems, other people can solve a myriad of problems.

Knowing the right person to call to get an answer or to solve a problem can make your life much easier.

Take the time to get to know the union steward, the payroll clerk, the person who handles medical claims, the storeroom custodian, the personnel officer and other people in key positions.

You'll find that they want to know you and will be happy to help you when you call. They are as proud of their work and ability to get things done as you are.

It will be time well invested.

> *"Knowing is of two kinds. We know a subject ourselves, or we know where we can find information upon it."*
> Samuel Johnson

MANAGE YOUR TIME

With increased responsibility, we should get increased time to carry out those responsibilities—but we don't!

You have three options:

Option 1: Use what time you do have to its maximum efficiency, carefully balancing between administration, supervision and time for your people. A difficult task, but then it goes with the title you've earned.

Option 2: Constantly be behind, late with deadlines, always behind on paperwork and not knowing what is going on. Of course if you choose this option, you will be a constant nervous wreck and probably not have a job very long.

Option 3: Significantly expand your workday. Work 12-14 hours every day—6 days a week and take work home with you every night—and some for Sunday, too. With this option, you'll keep your job—but probably lose your spouse, family, personal identity and have a heart attack at a young age.

Obviously you prefer Option 1. Even with Option 1, there will be times when you have to put in long days or take work home, but if you plan your time efficiently, they will be few.

"Work expands so as to fill the time available for its completion."

Northcote Parkinson
(Parkinson's Law)

❦ EPILOGUE

*I*f you have learned one new idea from reading the preceding pages, you are closer to success as a supervisor.

However, it should readily be recognized that there is a great deal more to supervision than the information contained in these few pages. This was but a prelude.

As you progress through your career, experience will be your best teacher and you will be its best student. The key is in your attitude.

Remember these four tenets if you remember nothing else and they will carry you on toward a successful and satisfying career.

1. Supervision is what *you* make of it.
2. Your people are your most valuable resource.
3. All problems can be handled.
4. People have faith in your abilities or you wouldn't be a supervisor.

Good Luck!

> *"Leadership is action, not position."*
> Donald H. McGannon

APPENDIX I

25 TRAITS OF EXCELLENT SUPERVISORS

1. Has Set Goals
2. Is Fair
3. Gives Positive Reinforcement
4. Is Knowledgeable
5. Respects Subordinates
6. Is Interested In Subordinates
7. Is Honest
8. Sets The Example
9. Has Common Sense
10. Is Decisive
11. Is A Teacher
12. Backs Subordinates' Decisions
13. Is A Good Listener
14. Delegates Work
15. Doesn't Monday Morning Quarterback
16. Is Available
17. Communicates Well
18. Is Responsible For Their Own Actions
19. Is Consistent
20. Is Willing To Help
21. Takes Command
22. Doesn't Hold Grudges
23. Show Enthusiasm For Their Work
24. Gives Constructive Feedback
25. Doesn't Overmanage

APPENDIX II

25 TRAITS OF POOR SUPERVISORS

1. Is Closed-minded
2. Is Two-faced
3. Doesn't Set A Good Example
4. Over-manages
5. Under-manages
6. Is Insensitive To Subordinates' Needs
7. Doesn't Have Respect For Subordinates
8. Is Inconsistent
9. Doesn't Accept Responsibility For Decisions
10. Is Arrogant
11. Lacks Experience
12. Takes Credit For Other's Work
13. Publicly Criticizes Subordinates
14. Shows Favoritism
15. Fails To Recognize Subordinates' Good Work
16. Is Indecisive
17. Holds Grudges
18. Communicates Poorly
19. Is Overly Critical
20. Is Lazy
21. Uses Power To Intimidate Subordinates
22. Is Insecure
23. Is Dishonest
24. Fails To Teach Subordinates
25. Fails To Back Subordinates' Decisions

APPENDIX III

25 COMMON MISTAKES MADE BY NEW SUPERVISORS

1. Made Changes For The Sake of Change
2. Immediately Made Drastic Changes In Discipline Or Procedures
3. Was Unable To Effectively Deal With People
4. Failed To Take Charge Of The Department
5. Made Serious Administrative Errors
6. Tried To Be "One Of The Guys"
7. Did Subordinates' Work For Them
8. Failed To Delegate
9. Gave No Positive Reinforcement To Subordinates
10. Had An Inconsistent Approach To Problems
11. Failed To Listen To Subordinates
12. Failed To Solicit Input From Subordinates
13. Showed Favoritism Among Subordinates
14. Failed To Motivate Subordinates
15. Didn't Address Problems Of Subordinates
16. Failed To Make Timely Decisions
17. Failed To Effectively Utilize Time
18. Lacked Communication Skills
19. Didn't Know Contents Of Required Paperwork
20. Failed To Foster Positive Interdepartmental Relations

21. Failed to Document Positive And Negative Activities of Subordinates
22. Gave Only Negative Criticism
23. Failed To Deal With Problems Immediately
24. Didn't Know When To Seek Advice From Or To Advise Superiors Of Problems
25. Lacked Knowledge of Labor Laws, Contracts Or Procedures

COMMON SENSE SUPERVISION is available directly from the publisher in individual and bulk quantities. For more information regarding discount schedules and ordering, please write:

> Ten Speed Press
> P.O. Box 7123
> Berkeley, California 94707

Roger Fulton has over 25 years of practical supervisory and leadership experience in both public and private sector organizations. He has studied the attributes of successful supervisors, managers, and leaders as an avocation, as well as for his own success. In addition to *Common Sense Supervision*, Mr. Fulton has published another book, *Common Sense Leadership*, as well as dozens of magazine and journal articles on the subject of management and supervision. Currently, he resides in Hayes, Virginia, where he is the President of Knight Management Corporation, a management training and consulting firm he founded in 1986.